Stars and Galaxies

PAUL HUMPHREY

TULIP
BOOKS

Tulip Books Limited

© 2019 Tulip Books Limited

Tulip Books
Suite LP33738
20-22 Wenlock Road
London N1 7GU

Series designed by Jurian Wiese
Book designed by Keith Williams, sprout.uk.com
Illustration on page 17 is by Keith Williams, sprout.uk.com

Production by Discovery Books

British Library Cataloguing in Publication Data
A full catalogue record for this book is available from the British Library

The publishers would like to thank the following for permission
to reproduce photographs:
Bigstock: Krisdog: 7;
NASA Images: title page; 3 (background); 14; 18 (inset); 19 (bottom); 21; 23
(background; 24 (background)
Shutterstock: Traveller Martin: 4-5; solarseven: 6; Baldas1950: 8; tatishdesign:
9; Aphelleon: 10; vectotatu: 11; Denis Belitsky: 12; Alex Mit: 13; Outer
Space: 15; RealCG Animation Studio: 16; LingHK: 18 (main image);
sciencepics 19 (top); freestyle images 20; Celig: 21

All the internet addresses (URLs) given in this book were valid at the time of
going to press. However, due to the dynamic nature of the internet, some
addresses may have changed, or sites may have changed or ceased to exist
since publication. While the author and publisher regret any inconvenience
this may cause readers, no responsibility for such changes can be accepted by
either the author or the publisher.

Printed by Melita
ISBN 978-1-78388-120-8

Contents

What is a Star?

Look up at the night sky. You will see thousands of twinkling lights. Most of these lights are distant stars. Stars are gigantic balls of very hot **gas**. They are found all over the **universe**.

DID YOU KNOW?

Distances in space are measured in light years. This is how far light travels in one year – nearly 10 trillion km.

Stars come in different shapes and sizes. They can be different colours too. Like living things, they have a **life cycle**, as we shall see.

The Sun, Our Star

Our Sun is the nearest star to Earth. Even so, it is still 150 million km away. The Sun brings light and warmth to the Earth. Without it, nothing could survive on our planet.

DID YOU KNOW?

The Sun is 1,391,400 km across, but some stars are much bigger than this!

Like all stars, the Sun is made up mostly of two gases. These are hydrogen and helium. Earth, and the other **planets** in the **solar system orbit** the Sun. They are all held in place by the Sun's pulling **force**, called **gravity**.

Constellations

Scientists, called **astronomers**, have studied the night sky for thousands of years. Ancient astronomers noticed that the stars seemed to form groups in the sky. They named these groups, or **constellations**, after people, animals and objects from their myths and legends.

DID YOU KNOW?

In 1922, the International Astronomical Union decided that there were 88 **constellations** in the night sky.

The constellations are useful because they help us to find other stars
in the sky. You can use a constellation called Ursa Major, or the
Great Bear, to find the Pole Star. Sailors used the Pole Star because
it lies above the **North Pole**. It helped them find their way at sea.

Galaxies

Galaxies are groups of stars. They are held together by the force of gravity. Some galaxies are small, with less than 1 million stars. Others are huge, and contain hundreds of billions of stars.

DID YOU KNOW?

Scientists believe that the universe and all the stars in it were born in a huge fireball. They think this happened 13.7 billion years ago.

GALAXY TYPES

Elliptical

Irregular

Spiral

Galaxies come in different shapes. **Spiral** galaxies look like spinning fireworks in the sky. **Elliptical** galaxies are oval-shaped, like a rugby ball. **Irregular** galaxies have no shape at all.

The Milky Way

Our Sun and solar system lie in a spiral galaxy called the Milky Way. The Milky Way contains at least 100 million stars. Our solar system is about 27,000 light years away from the centre of the Milky Way.

Milky Way

All the stars and planets of the Milky Way orbit the centre of the galaxy. It takes 225 million years for a star to make one orbit.

DID YOU KNOW?

The astronomer Galileo was the first person to discover that the Milky Way was made up of thousands of stars.

Birth of a Star

Stars don't shine forever. They are born, grow old and, eventually, die. But don't worry about our Sun. The life cycle of a star can last billions of years, and our Sun has a lot of life left in it yet.

The Helix Nebula

Stars are born in a dusty cloud called a **nebula**. First, the bits of dust and gases start to join together. Gravity squeezes everything and makes the gas heat up. The star starts to shine.

The Carina Nebula

DID YOU KNOW?

Our Sun will probably shine for another 5 billion years.

DID YOU KNOW?

Proxima Centuari is the nearest star to our solar system. It is just 4.2 light years from the Sun.

Life of Star

Stars come in many shapes and sizes. They can go on burning for many billions of years. Some are very hot, up to 35,000°C. The surface of our Sun is just over 5,500°C.

Stars like our Sun are in balance. The force of gravity is pushing the star in on itself, like squeezing a sponge. Meanwhile **pressure** from the centre, or **core**, of the Sun is pushing outwards, like a balloon blowing up.

Gravity pushes inwards

Pressure from the core pushes outwards

When the two forces on a star are equal, the star is in balance.

Death of a Star

Eventually, stars run out of the gases they use for fuel. The star may then expand into a huge star called a red giant. One day, our own Sun will turn into a red giant. Then it will be 30 times bigger and 1,000 times brighter than it is today.

Or the star might blow up in a giant explosion, called a **supernova**.

Eventually, the star turns into a white dwarf star. Gravity pulls all the bits of the star into a very **dense** core.

DID YOU KNOW?

There is a black hole at the centre of the Milky Way.

The star may even turn into a black hole. This is a star that is so dense that nothing can escape the pull of its gravity, not even light.

Exploring the Stars

Travelling to the stars will not be easy. Our fastest spacecraft can travel at almost 58,000 kph. But, even at this speed, it would take them thousands of years to reach the nearest star.

For the time being, we will have to be satisfied with just looking at the stars from Earth, or from space **telescopes**. The Hubble Space Telescope was launched in 1990. It has sent us some amazing photographs of galaxies and nebulae.

DID YOU KNOW?

In 2019, the James Webb Space Telescope will be launched. This will be even more powerful than Hubble.

Stargazing

You can see the stars and constellations just by using your eyes. But if you want a closer look, you'll need a pair of binoculars, or better still, a telescope. When choosing a telescope, you need to find out its **aperture**. This is the size of the lens that collects the light. This needs to be at least 70mm.

You need to go somewhere where there is no other light from street lamps and buildings. And, of course, you need a starry night, with little moonlight and no clouds.

Glossary

aperture the diameter (distance across) a lens in a telescope or camera

astronomer a person who studies the stars, planets and outer space

constellation a group of stars

core the centre of something

dense closely packed together

elliptical oval-shaped, like a rugby ball

force a push or pull on an object

galaxy a very large group of stars and planets

gas a substance, such as air, that will expand to fill any space that contains it

gravity the force that pulls objects towards each other in space and also pulls things towards the centre of a star or a planet, like Earth

irregular describes something that has no fixed shape

life cycle a series of changes that something goes through from birth to death

nebula (plural nebulae) a bright, cloudlike mass in the night sky that is made up of stars or gases and dust

North Pole the most northern point on Earth

orbit the path of one object in space around another, like the Earth around the Sun

planet one of the heavenly bodies (very large objects) that orbit the Sun or other stars in space

pressure a force produced by pressing on something

solar system the planets, rocks, ice and other debris that orbit a star

spiral a spiral pattern winds around and around itself, like a spring

supernova an extremely bright, exploding star

telescope an instrument that makes distant objects seem closer

universe the Earth, Sun and planets and all the other things that exist in space

Further Information

Books

50 Things You Should Know About Space by Professor Raman Prinja, QED Publishing, 2016

Stars and Galaxies by James Buckley Jnr, DK Readers, 2017

Galaxies and Stars by Ian Graham, Franklin Watts 2016

Stars, Galaxies and the Milky Way by Clive Gifford, Wayland, 2015

100 Facts Stars and Galaxies by Clive Gifford, Miles Kelly Ltd, 2015

Websites

NASA Kids' Club:
https://www.nasa.gov/kidsclub/index.html

European Space Agency:
https://www.esa.int/esaKIDSen/

Places to Visit

The London Planetarium, Marylebone Road, London, England

The Sydney Observatory, 1003 Upper Fort St Millers Point NSW, Sydney, New South Wales, Australia

Index